Clara Schumann

Piano Music

Selected and with an Introduction by
Nancy B. Reich

DOVER PUBLICATIONS, INC.
Mineola, New York

Bibliographical Note

This Dover edition, first published in 2000, is a new compilation of piano works by Clara Schumann originally published separately in authoritative early editions. Dr. Nancy B. Reich has written her introduction specially for this edition, and corrected a few obvious errors in the original plates without further comment.

We are grateful to Dr. Reich and to the Duke University Music Library for providing rare copies of the music reproduced in this collection.

International Standard Book Number
ISBN-13: 978-0-486-41381-5
ISBN-10: 0-486-41381-0

Manufactured in the United States by Courier Corporation
41381004
www.doverpublications.com

INTRODUCTION

Clara Wieck Schumann (1819–1896), a leading pianist of the 19th century, was also a respected published composer during her lifetime. As an 18-year-old, she was regarded by her contemporaries as a member of the avant-garde "new romantic" school, and her works were praised and performed by such musicians as Chopin, Brahms, Mendelssohn, Liszt and Joachim. Today, in the wake of a feminist movement that is rediscovering creative women, Clara Schumann's music is being heard again: newly uncovered pieces have been published; over 100 recordings of her music are available; and her songs and piano works are heard on radio and in concert halls the world over.

Clara Wieck was a child prodigy and adolescent star, dazzling audiences in her native Leipzig, and in Paris, Berlin and Vienna with her playing and her compositions. Her father, Friedrich Wieck—piano teacher and piano merchant— was her sole teacher, becoming her concert manager as well when he realized the scope of her amazing talents and earning potential. However, father and daughter parted ways when Clara declared her intention to marry Robert Schumann, then little more than a poor, unrecognized composer.

After a long, tempestuous legal battle with her father, Clara married Robert in 1840, and continued to perform and compose during the sixteen years of their marriage. In 1856 her husband passed away after a prolonged and troubled illness, leaving Clara, at age 37, to support her family of seven children (the youngest was but two years old). Out of necessity, Clara Schumann abandoned composition to return to the concert stage.

THE COMPOSITIONS

• A great favorite with the public, "Hexentanz" (Witches Dance)—the first of *Quatre Pièces caractéristiques,* Op. 5—was composed before Clara's marriage and first published in 1836 as "Impromptu. Le Sabbat." In the spring of 1838, while Clara and her father were on a triumphant Viennese concert tour, the piece was reissued by Haslinger, Vienna, as "Hexentanz."

• Opus 15, *Quatre Pièces fugitives,* was first published in 1845 but given the German title *Vier flüchtige Stücke* in a collection of Clara Schumann's piano music published in 1879 by Breitkopf & Härtel (see the note at the end of this text). This elusive title suggests the English version offered here: *Four Fleeting Pieces.*

• The *Three Preludes and Fugues,* Op. 16, were written and published in 1845. "Studying fugues diligently with Clara," wrote Robert Schumann in his diary in February 1845. He was proud of his wife's skills, declaring to one publisher that this was probably the first time that a woman had attempted "this beautiful but difficult genre," and writing to a friend, "I am also sending you the fugues of my Clara; I admit to being very fond of them."

• Clara Schumann rarely performed her own compositions in public; however, her *Variations on a Theme by Robert Schumann,* Op. 20, was an exception, appearing on her concert programs for Rotterdam, Leipzig, Vienna and London.

The birth of this work was announced in her diary for May 29, 1853: "Today I began to compose again for the first time in several years; I want to work on variations on a theme from his *Bunte Blätter* [Colored Leaves, Op. 99] for Robert for his birthday; it is very hard for me, however—I have paused too long." The theme she chose was from the first of five *Albumblätter* [Album Leaves].

Appearing the next year, 1854, after Robert was hospitalized, Clara's *Variations* recalled earlier, happier days, even quoting a theme (mm. 202–225) from her own *Romance variée,* Op. 3. That work of 1833 was the music on which Robert had based *his* Op. 5 variations, *Impromptus on a Romance of Clara Wieck.*

Clara Schumann's Op. 20 had further repercussions, for Johannes Brahms—the young, then unknown composer the Schumanns had befriended—proceeded to compose variations on the same Robert Schumann theme after studying Clara's unpublished score. Penned on the manuscript of Brahms's Opus 9 is an inscription reflecting the closeness of these three musicians: "Little variations on a theme by him/dedicated to her."

• The *Romance,* Op. 11, No. 2—completed while Clara was in Paris in 1839—first appeared as *Andante und Allegro* in the September 1839 musical supplement to the *Neue Zeitschrift für Musik,* the music journal edited by Robert Schumann. The next year, the entire opus 11 was published in Vienna by Mechetti, as *Trois Romances.* (The present volume reprints the Mechetti edition.)

• Clara Schumann began her *Three Romances,* Op. 21, in June 1853, but replaced the first piece two years later with another (also in A minor), composed in April 1855 on a day that her devoted friend Johannes Brahms was visiting Robert in the hospital. Her "little pieces," as she called them, were dedicated to Brahms. The set was published that same year.

Many of Clara Schumann's published piano works have been reissued in recent years, but as of this writing the present Dover edition is the first known modern reprint of Opp. 15, 16, 20 and 21 brought together in a single volume. These originated in *Pianoforte-Werke zu 2 Händen von Clara Schumann,* a collection published by Breitkopf & Härtel, Leipzig, in 1879. This particular album is of special interest because it includes all the late piano works with opus numbers published during her lifetime, although Breitkopf did not use all the original plates.

We assume that the composer (then 60 years old and in full career) gave permission for this collection, but may have been too preoccupied to proofread the new set carefully, as was her custom. It was issued just about the time that two of her adult children were ill, two had died, she had begun a new teaching position, and was embarking on her edition of the complete *Robert Schumann Werke* for Breitkopf. The few errors that crept into the plates have been corrected here without comment.

Finally, the works in this collection represent but a small part of the oeuvre of Clara Wieck Schumann. Among her other compositions are a strikingly innovative piano concerto, a masterful piano trio, and a number of dramatic and impressive songs. Musicians and music lovers will be well rewarded by knowledge of her works.

Nancy B. Reich

Hastings-on-Hudson, New York
Summer 2000

Dr. Reich is a leading authority on the life and works of Clara Schumann. Her book, *Clara Schumann: The Artist and the Woman,* was published by Cornell University Press, 1985; a revised edition is scheduled to appear in 2001.

CONTENTS

Witches Dance

Op. 5, No. 1

mf
Ped.
sf
ff
p
cresc.
poco a poco
f

ff Ped.
sf
f Ped.
Ped.
ff Ped.
Ped.
Ped.
sf
ff Ped.
Ped.
f
poco a poco
dimi
nu
en
do.
1° Ped.
Ped.
mf Ped.
Ped.

sf
Ped.
sf
Ped.
sf
Ped.
sf
Ped.
Ped.
sf
dim.
pp
Ped
Ped
f
Ped.
Ped.
dimin.
p
Ped
Ped
sf
Ped.
p
Ped.
p
Ped.
Ped.
sf
Ped.
p
Ped.
p
Ped.
cresc.
sf
ff
Ped.
sf
sf

Dedicated to her sister Marie Wieck

Four Fleeting Pieces

Op. 15

p
pp
ri - tar - dan - - do
p
un poco animato
Ped.
cresc.
p
pp
ritard.
Ped.

Un poco agitato. ♩. = 108
No. 2
p
Ped.
cresc.
Ped
rit.
a tempo
cresc.

dim.
cresc.
f
f
cresc.
p
dim.
pp

Ped
cresc.
p
pp
dim.

Andante espressivo.
No. 3
p
cresc.
p
dim.
p
cresc.
mf
diminuendo
un poco più animato

pp
cresc
poco
cresc.
f
f
p
mf
cresc.
ril.
dim.
p
pp
rile
nuto

Tempo I°
p
mf
p
diminuendo
p
p
mf
p
poco diminuendo
poco a poco ritardando

No. 4
Scherzo. 𝅗𝅥. = 96
p
Ped.
cresc.
1a
2a
Un poco più tranquillo
p
mf

cresc.
Ped.
Ped.
mf
ritenuto
p
I° Tempo.
p
Ped.
dim.
f

Three Preludes and Fugues

Op. 16

Praeludium I

Fuga I

Allegro vivace.

f
f
f
f

Praeludium II

dim.
p
mf
cresc.
dimin.
Ped.
attacca Fuga

Fuga II

Praeludium III

ritard.
attacca Fuga

Fuga III

Fine.

Variations on a Theme by Robert Schumann

Op. 20

cresc.
p
pp
Var. II
p
cresc.

p
cresc.
f
legato.
mf

calando
p
Var. III
p
dim.
cresc.
dim.
pp

Var. IV
p
mf
sf

sf
dim.
8
8
dim.
sosten.

Poco animato.
Var. V
f
sf
p
cresc.
sf
f
mf

cresc.
Das 1te Mal.
Das 2te Mal.
f
Var. VI
p
cresc.
sf
calando
p
pp

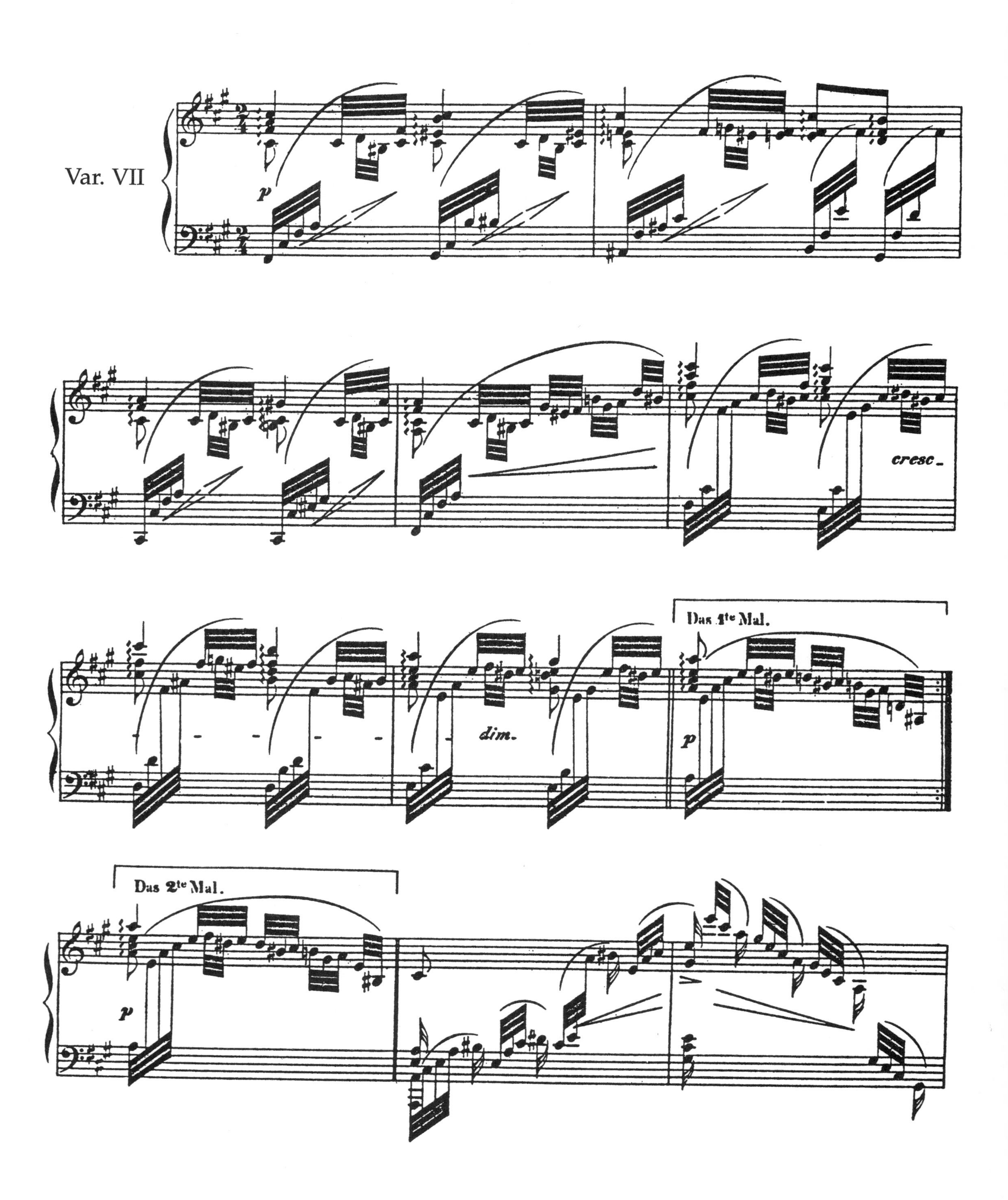
Var. VII
p
cresc.
dim.
Das 1te Mal.
p
Das 2te Mal.
p

cresc.
sf
sosten.
f
p
ritard.
dim.

molto espressivo.
pp
cresc.
f
dim.
8
rit.
p
cresc.
dim.

pp
calando
p
cresc.
stretto
dim.
ritenuto.
ppp
8
Ped.

Romance

Op. 11, No. 2

Nach und nach schneller.
p
f
ritardando.
ff
p
ritardando.

Allegro passionato.
p
ritardando.
f
f
sf
sf
p
p

Tempo, wie zu Anfang.
p
f
p
8a loco.
sf
sf
sf
8a loco.
ritard:
f

p
pp
8a
sf
ri - - tar - - dan - - - do
Adagio.
sf
ri - - tar - - dan - - do.
pp
pp

Dedicated with friendship to Johannes Brahms

Three Romances

Op. 21

Romance No. 1

Sehr innig bewegt.
animato
p
cresc.
Ped.
cresc.
Ped.
p
cresc.
calando.
pp
Ped.
ritenuto.
p
a tempo.
cresc.

f
sf
sf
mf
cresc.
dim.
p
cresc.
Ped.
mf
poco
a
poco
dimi
nu
en
do
calando
Ped.

Tempo I.
p
cresc.
cresc.
sf
f
ff
strin - gen - do
sf
dimin.
p
pp

Romance No. 2

cresc.
Ped.
Ped.
p

cresc.
f
dim.
Ped.
p

p
calando
dim.
a tempo.
p

Romance No. 3

cresc.
f
cresc.
Ped.
dim.
Ped.
Ped.
p

calando
rit.
Ped.

Langsamer.
p
Ped.
Ped.
Ped.
Ped.
cresc.
rit.
a tempo.
pp rit.
mf
a tempo.
cresc.
cresc.

Tempo I.
p
dim.
p

cresc.
f
cresc.
Ped.
dimin.
Ped.
Ped.
p

END OF EDITION